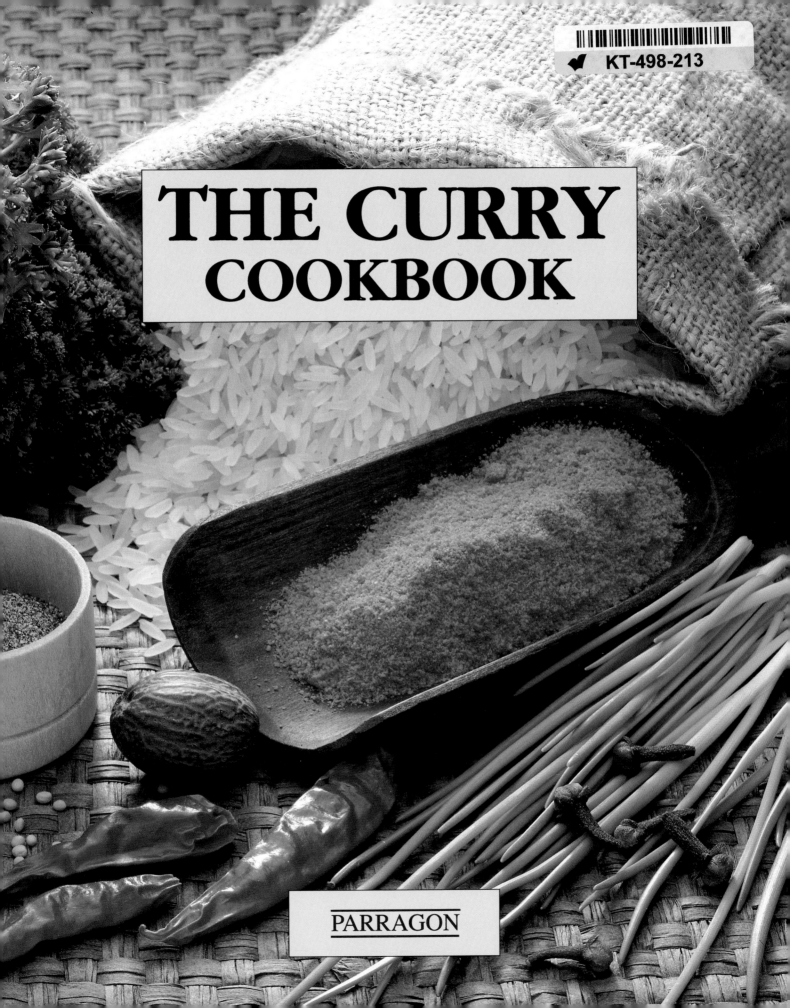

THE CURRY
COOKBOOK

PARRAGON

THE CURRY
COOKBOOK

Photography by Peter Barry
Designed by Richard Hawke and Claire Leighton
Edited by Jillian Stewart and Kate Cranshaw
Recipes by Judith Ferguson, Lalita Ahmed and
    Carolyn Garner

3450
© 1993 Coombe Books
This edition published in 1994 by Coombe Books for
Parragon Book Service Ltd
Unit 13-17, Avonbridge Trading Estate
Atlantic Road, Avonmouth, Bristol BS11 9QD
All rights reserved
Printed and bound in Hong Kong
ISBN 1-85813-376-9

Contents

Introduction

The curry is well known as the staple cuisine of India, but probably less well known is its influence on the cooking of other Far Eastern countries such as Thailand, Malaysia, Java, and Indonesia. These countries have adopted the curry and given it a new lease of life by adding some of their own flavourings. A typical Thai curry might contain, for example, spices ground up with fresh coriander, lemon grass, chillies and garlic; and seasonings such as fish sauce, shrimp paste, tamarind, citrus juice and palm sugar.

In India, curries are traditionally cooked in a deep straight-sided pot called a *degchi*, and strictly speaking a curry is simply a dish with a sauce. A curry is made up of several elements; a combination of spices, herbs and aromatics; the main bulk ingredient such as meat or vegetables; and liquid to make the sauce. The seasonings and sauce ingredients differ from region to region, due to climate, terrain and the past influences of invading countries. In the north, for example, *garam masala* often provides the basic flavouring with cream or yogurt added to the sauce to give it a smooth, thick texture. The south uses more fresh seasoning ingredients such as coriander, fenugreek, mint and ginger, and in contrast uses coconut milk, rather than yogurt, to thicken sauces.

Varying accompaniments can be served with a curry; a rice dish is the first obvious choice – either plain boiled rice or a pilau rice; and a bread such as naan or chapatti is also popular. When a meal is served in India, the variety of dishes served is far greater as it is considered correct to balance the meal between hot and cool, and dry and wet dishes. A hot dish would be balanced by serving a cooling accompaniment such as a *raita* (a cooling milk or curd preparation), and a curry dish would be complemented with a dry vegetable side dish. Other accompaniments could include some *anchars* (fresh pickles), *sambals* (pungent finely ground mixtures of fish, meat, or vegetables), *cachombars* (fresh mixed vegetables with herbs); and a salad or fresh vegetable chutney.

Many of the spices used in this book are now commonly available in most large supermarkets. Some of the Thai ingredients such as shrimp paste and fish sauce may be less familiar, but many of these are now also available in good supermarkets as well as speciality stores. Traditionally, the quantities used in Indian cooking were not measured and recipes were passed down from one generation to the next with all the quantities being estimated. Thankfully for us, these recipes have been quantified to make life much simpler, however everyone has their own tastes, and much of the joy of making curries is experimenting and developing your own favourites to entertain friends and family.

Sweet Bean Curry

This excellent curry will freeze well for up to six weeks.

SERVES 4

175g/6oz red kidney beans, soaked overnight
30g/1oz butter or margarine
1 onion, sliced
1 apple, cored and chopped
175g/6oz mushrooms, sliced
1 tbsp curry powder
30g/1oz flour
570ml/1 pint bean stock or bean stock and water
Salt to taste
1 tbsp lemon juice
1 tbsp chutney
60g/2oz sultanas
60g/2oz creamed coconut, grated or chopped

1. Drain the beans, put into a large pan and cover with cold water.

2. Bring to the boil and boil vigorously for 10-15 minutes, turn down the heat and boil for about 1 hour until the beans are tender but still whole. Drain and reserve the liquid.

3. Melt the butter or margarine and cook the onion until it is very brown.

4. Add the apple and mushrooms and cook for 2-3 minutes.

5. Add the curry powder and flour and cook for a couple of minutes, stirring all the time.

6. Gradually add 570ml/1 pint bean liquid, make up with water if necessary, and stir until smooth.

7. Add the seasoning, lemon juice, chutney, sultanas and beans and cook for 10-15 minutes.

8. Just before serving add the creamed coconut and stir until dissolved.

TIME: Preparation takes 25 minutes plus overnight soaking of the beans. Cooking time, including the beans, 1 hour 35 minutes.

SERVING IDEAS: Serve with boiled brown rice and fried plantains – peel, cut into 1.2cm/½-inch slices and fry in hot oil until golden brown. If unavailable you can use unripe green bananas. Garnish the curry with quarters of hard-boiled eggs.

LENTIL AND VEGETABLE CURRY

*Lentils are a staple ingredient in Indian cookery. This delicious vegetable curry
should be made using fresh spices for the best flavour.*

SERVES 4

225g/8oz whole green lentils
2 tbsps vegetable oil
½ tsp mustard seed, crushed
1 tsp ground coriander
½ tsp ground cumin
2 dried red chillies, crushed
1 carrot, peeled and diagonally sliced
1 potato, peeled and cubed
6-8 okra, topped and tailed, then cut into
    2.5cm/1-inch pieces
1 small courgette, diagonally sliced
1 small aubergine, halved and sliced
430ml/¾ pint water
6 curry leaves
1 green chilli, slit in half and chopped
1 tsp fresh chopped mint
1 tbsp fresh chopped coriander
Salt to taste
Coriander leaves to garnish

1. Wash the lentils in warm water until it
runs clear. Drain well.

2. Put the lentils into a large saucepan and
pour over 570ml/1 pint water. Simmer
gently for 15-20 minutes.

3. When the lentils are soft, beat with a
potato masher or whisk until they are
puréed.

4. In a large saucepan heat the oil and
gently fry the mustard seed, ground coriander, cumin and dried chillies for 1
minute.

5. Add the vegetables to the spices and
cook for 2 minutes, stirring all the time, to
coat them evenly in the oil and spice
mixture.

6. Add the water and the puréed lentils to
the vegetable mixture and stir well.

7. Add the curry leaves, chopped chilli,
mint, fresh coriander and salt, then cook for
15 minutes. Serve hot, garnished with coriander leaves.

TIME: Preparation takes about 10 minutes, cooking takes 35-40 minutes.

VARIATION: Use any combination of fresh vegetables to vary this curry.

SERVING IDEAS: Serve with boiled basmati rice.

MIXED VEGETABLE CURRY

A variety of seasonal vegetables are cooked together in a gravy flavoured by a few ground spices, onions and tomatoes. Whole green chillies are added towards the end to enhance the flavour of the dish and also to retain their fresh green colour.

SERVES 4-6

60-75ml/4-5 tbsps cooking oil

1 large onion, finely chopped

1.25cm/½-inch cube of fresh root ginger, peeled and finely sliced

1 tsp ground turmeric

1 tsp ground coriander

1 tsp ground cumin

1 tsp paprika

4 small ripe tomatoes, skinned and chopped or a small can of tomatoes with the juice

225g/8oz potatoes, peeled and diced

90g/3oz french beans or dwarf beans, sliced

120g/4oz carrots, sliced

90g/3oz garden peas, shelled weight

430ml/¾ pint warm water

2-4 whole fresh green chillies

1 tsp garam masala

1 tsp salt or to taste

1 tbsp chopped coriander leaves

1. Heat the oil over a medium heat and cook the onion for 6-7 minutes until lightly browned.

2. Add the ginger and fry for 30 seconds.

3. Over a low heat, add the turmeric, coriander, cumin and paprika. Stir and mix well.

4. Add half the tomatoes and cook for 2 minutes, stirring continuously.

5. Add all the vegetables and the water. Stir and mix well. Bring to the boil, cover and simmer for 15-20 minutes, or until the vegetables are tender.

6. Add the remaining tomatoes and the green chillies. Cover and simmer for 5-6 minutes.

7. Add the garam masala and salt, mix well. Stir in half the coriander leaves and remove from heat.

8. Put the vegetable curry into a heated serving dish and sprinkle the remaining coriander leaves on top.

TIME: Preparation takes 25-30 minutes, cooking takes 30 minutes.

SERVING IDEAS: Serve with naan bread, Indian chutney, and plain boiled rice.

TO FREEZE: Suitable for freezing, but omit the potatoes. Add pre-boiled diced potatoes during reheating.

WATCHPOINT: Frozen peas and beans may be used for convenience, but the cooking time should be adjusted accordingly. Cook the fresh vegetables first and follow cooking time for frozen vegetables as per instructions on packets.

GREEN LENTILS WITH FRESH GINGER AND SPICES

There's certainly no lack of taste in this spicy lentil mix.

SERVES 4

175g/6oz green or Continental lentils

Water or stock to cover

30g/1oz margarine or 1 tbsp oil

1 medium onion, finely chopped

2.5cm/1-inch piece fresh root ginger,
    peeled and grated

1 tsp garam masala

1 tsp cumin seeds

1 tsp coriander seeds, crushed

1 tsp green cardamom pods, seeds removed
    and crushed

1 medium carrot, diced

1 × 400g/14oz can peeled tomatoes

60g/2oz mushrooms, finely chopped

1 tbsp shoyu sauce (Japanese soy sauce)

1 tbsp cider vinegar

Salt and freshly ground black pepper to
    taste

Lemon slices and freshly chopped parsley
    or coriander to garnish

1. Pick over the lentils and wash thoroughly.

2. Place in a large, heavy-based saucepan, cover with water or stock and bring to the boil. Turn off the heat, cover and leave to begin to swell.

3. Meanwhile, heat the margarine or oil in a separate saucepan and gently fry the onion, ginger and spices until they are well combined, and aromatic.

4. Add to the lentils, bring to the boil and start to add the other vegetables, allowing several minutes between each addition, beginning with the carrot followed by the tomatoes and lastly the chopped mushrooms.

5. Stir frequently to prevent sticking and check on liquid quantity regularly, adding more water or stock as necessary.

6. Just before the end of the cooking time – approximately 25 minutes depending on the age of the lentils – add the shoyu, cider vinegar and salt and pepper.

7. Cook for a few more minutes and serve hot garnished with slices of lemon and freshly chopped parsley or coriander.

TIME: Preparation takes about 25 minutes, cooking takes about 45 minutes.

SERVING IDEAS: Serve with boiled wholegrain rice and salad made from beansprouts, red and green pappers and grated daikon.

VARIATION: Black olives can replace the chopped parsley or coriander.

RED KIDNEY BEAN CURRY

A popular dish from the Punjab province of India. It is similar to Chilli Con-Carne and makes a hearty meal with bread or rice.

SERVES 4

225g/8oz dried red kidney beans, washed and soaked overnight in sufficient water to cover
2 medium onions, chopped
3 tbsps oil
1 bayleaf
2.5cm/1-inch piece cinnamon stick
6 cloves
6 small green cardamoms
2 green chillies, quartered
3 cloves garlic, finely chopped
2.5cm/1-inch fresh root ginger, peeled and finely chopped
½ tsp chilli powder
¼ tsp ground turmeric
1½ tsps ground coriander
1 tsp ground cumin
1 tsp garam masala powder
400g/14oz can peeled tomatoes, chopped
½ tsp salt
2-3 sprigs fresh green coriander, chopped

1. Cook the kidney beans in their soaking water for 15-20 minutes, or until soft. Remove from the heat; allow to stand, covered.

2. Fry the onions in the oil in a large saucepan over a moderate heat until tender.

3. Add the bayleaf, cinnamon, cloves and cardamoms and fry for 1 minute.

4. Add the chillies, garlic and ginger and fry until golden. Sprinkle with the chilli powder, turmeric, ground coriander, ground cumin and garam masala.

5. Stir the mixture well to blend the spices. Do not allow the mixture to burn.

6. Add the tomatoes and season with salt. Cover and simmer for 2-3 minutes.

7. Drain the cooked beans and collect the thick cooking liquid. Add the beans to the spiced tomato mixture. Stir gently and cook for 1 minute.

8. Add the cooking liquid and chopped coriander, cover and simmer for 3-5 minutes, then serve.

TIME: Preparation takes 15 minutes, plus overnight soaking for the beans. Cooking takes about 40 minutes.

COOK'S TIP: To reduce the cooking time, cook the kidney beans in a pressure cooker for 5-6 minutes at 15lbs pressure.

SERVING IDEAS: Serve with naan bread or boiled rice.

FISH SHAHJAHANI

This rich, but easy to prepare fish dish is named after the Mughal Emperor Shah-jahan, who was noted for his love of good food.

SERVES 4

675g/1½lbs fillet of any white fish
90g/3oz roasted cashews
120ml/4 fl oz single cream
60g/2oz ghee or unsalted butter
225g/8oz onions, finely sliced
5cm/2-inch piece of cinnamon stick, broken
4 green cardamoms, split open at the top of
    each pod
2 whole cloves
1-2 fresh green chillies, sliced lengthwise;
    seeded if a milder flavour is preferred
1 tsp ground turmeric
175ml/6 fl oz warm water
1 tsp salt or to taste
1 tbsp lemon juice

1. Rinse the fish gently in cold water, dry on kitchen paper and cut into 2.5 × 5cm/1 × 2-inch pieces.

2. Put the cashews and the cream into an electric blender and blend to a reasonably fine mixture.

3. In a wide, shallow pan melt the ghee or butter over a medium heat and fry onions, cinnamon, cardamom, cloves and green chillies for 6-8 minutes, until the onions are lightly browned. Stir in the turmeric.

4. Add the water and salt and arrange the fish in a single layer. Bring to the boil, cover the pan and simmer for 2-3 minutes.

5. Now add the cashew/cream mixture and stir gently until the pieces of fish are well coated. Cover the pan again and simmer for a further 2-3 minutes.

6. Remove from the heat and gently stir in the lemon juice.

TIME: Preparation takes 15 minutes, cooking takes 15-20 minutes.

SERVING IDEAS: To appreciate the wonderful flavour of this dish fully, the rice served with it should not be too highly flavoured.

VARIATION: Use potatoes which have been boiled in their jackets, peeled and diced

WATCHPOINT: It is important to use a wide shallow pan so that the fish can be arranged in a single layer to prevent them from breaking up during cooking.

Prawns in Green Curry Paste

This is the hottest of Thai curries because of the large number of small green Serrano chillies traditionally used.

SERVES 2-3

Green Curry Paste

10 green Serrano or other small chillies, chopped
3 cloves garlic, crushed
2 stems lemon grass, roughly chopped
3 spring onions, chopped
1 tsp grated ginger
1 tsp coriander seeds
1 tsp caraway seeds
4 whole cloves
1 tsp ground nutmeg
1 tsp shrimp paste
3 tbsps oil

Curry

200ml/7 fl oz thick coconut milk
2 tbsps green curry paste
340g/12oz peeled, raw prawns
1 tbsp fish sauce
Zested lemon rind to garnish

1. Make the curry paste by placing all the ingredients in a food processor and grinding to a paste. Store in a small jar in the refrigerator until required.

2. Heat a little of the coconut milk in a wok and add the 2 tbsp curry paste, boil rapidly for 5 minutes, stirring frequently, then reduce the heat.

3. Gradually stir in the remaining coconut milk, then add the prawns and fish sauce. Cook gently for about 5 minutes until prawns are cooked.

4. Garnish with lemon rind and serve with steamed rice.

TIME: Preparation takes 15 minutes and cooking takes 10 minutes.

COOK'S TIP: The paste will keep for up to 1 month if stored in an airtight jar in the refrigerator.

PREPARATION: To use the lemon grass, remove the tough dry outer leaves before chopping the soft inner core

PRAWN CHILLI MASALA

This is a delicate but richly flavoured dish. In India, only fresh and juicy king prawns will do, but standard peeled prawns can be used for this recipe.

SERVES 4

90g/3oz ghee or unsalted butter

6 green cardamoms, split open at the top of each pod

2.5cm/1-inch cube of root ginger, peeled and finely grated

3-4 cloves garlic, crushed

1 tbsp ground coriander

½ tsp ground turmeric

450g/1lb fresh peeled prawns

150g/5oz thick set natural yogurt

90ml/3 fl oz water

1 tsp sugar

1 tsp salt or to taste

30g/1oz ground almonds

4-6 whole fresh green chillies

1 large onion, finely sliced

2 fresh green chillies, seeded and very finely chopped

½ tsp garam masala

1 tbsp chopped coriander leaves

1. Melt 60g/2oz of the ghee or butter over a gentle heat and add the whole cardamoms, fry for 30 seconds and add the ginger and garlic. Stir and cook for 1 minute, then add the ground coriander and turmeric. Stir and fry for 30 seconds.

2. Add the prawns, turn the heat up to medium and cook for 5-6 minutes, stirring frequently.

3. Beat the yogurt until smooth, gradually add the water and beat until well blended. Add this mixture to the prawns, stir in the sugar and the salt, cover the pan and simmer for 5-6 minutes.

4. Add the ground almonds and the whole green chillies and cook, uncovered, for 5 minutes.

5. Meanwhile, fry the onion in the remaining ghee until it is just soft, but not brown. Add the finely chopped green chillies and the garam masala; stir and fry for a further 1-2 minutes. Stir this mixture into the prawns along with any ghee left in the pan. Remove the pan from the heat.

6. Put the prawns into a serving dish and garnish with the coriander leaves.

TIME: Preparation takes 15 minutes, cooking takes 20-25 minutes.

SERVING IDEAS: Serve with Pilau Rice and a side dish.

FISH BHOONA

SERVES 4

675g/1½lbs steaks or fillets of any white fish
90ml/6 tbsps cooking oil

Mix the following 4 ingredients in a small bowl
1 tbsp plain flour
¼ tsp ground turmeric
¼ tsp chilli powder
¼ tsp salt

1 large onion, coarsely chopped
1.25cm/½-inch cube of fresh root ginger, peeled and coarsely chopped
2-4 cloves garlic, coarsely chopped
½ tsp ground turmeric
¼ tsp chilli powder
1 tsp ground coriander
½ tsp garam masala
1 small can of tomatoes
150ml/5 fl oz warm water
120g/4oz frozen garden peas
1 tsp salt or to taste
1 tbsp chopped coriander leaves

1. Skin the fish, wash and dry thoroughly on kitchen paper and cut the fish into approximately 2.5 × 5cm/1-× 2-inch pieces.

2. Heat 2 tbsps of the oil in a large frying pan, preferably non-stick or cast iron, over a medium heat.

3. Lightly dust the fish, one piece at a time, in the seasoned flour and place in the hot oil. Put in as many pieces as the pan will hold in a single layer without overcrowding it and adjust heat to medium-high. Fry the fish until all the pieces are evenly browned. This has to be done quickly in fairly hot oil so that the fish is thoroughly sealed. Drain on kitchen paper.

4. Put the onion, ginger and garlic into a liquidiser or food processor and blend until smooth.

5. Heat the remaining oil over a medium heat in a wide, shallow pan. Add the onion mixture and stir. When the mixture is heated through turn heat down to low, stir and fry for 3-4 minutes.

6. Add the turmeric, chilli, coriander and garam masala and fry for 4-5 minutes. Stir continuously, adding 1 tbsp juice from the can of tomatoes from time to time to prevent the spices from sticking to the bottom of the pan.

7. Now add one tomato at a time, along with any remaining juice, breaking the tomatoes up with the back of the spoon. Cook until the tomatoes are well incorporated into the rest of the ingredients.

8. Add the water, peas and salt. Bring to the boil and add the fish. Cover and simmer for 5-6 minutes.

9. Remove from heat and sprinkle the coriander leaves on top.

TIME: Preparation takes 15-20 minutes, cooking takes 30-35 minutes.

CURRIED PRAWNS

This prawn curry could be served as a starter or as a main course.

SERVES 4 or 8

2 tbsps oil
2 onions, finely sliced
2 cloves garlic, crushed
½ tsp chilli powder
½ tsp ground mace
2 tsp ground coriander
1 tsp ground turmeric
1 tsp grated ginger
900g/2lbs uncooked, peeled prawns
Juice of 1 lime
430ml/¾ pint coconut milk
Salt and pepper
1 small fresh ripe pineapple, peeled, cored
     and cut into chunks
1 banana, peeled and thinly sliced
60g/2oz roasted, unsalted cashew nuts

1. Heat the oil in wok or frying pan and add the onions and garlic and cook until lightly browned.

2. Add the ground spices and ginger and stir-fry for 1-2 minutes.

3. Add the prawns and stir-fry for 1 minute.

4. Add the lime juice and coconut milk and season with salt and pepper.

5. Stir well and cook gently for about 10 minutes until the prawns are cooked.

6. Add the pineapple, banana and cashews and stir carefully. Cook a further 1-2 minutes to heat all the ingredients through.

TIME: Preparation takes about 20 minutes and cooking takes 14-15 minutes.
VARIATION: Use king prawns and cook for slightly longer.

CURRY PARCELS

A tasty snack which can be served any time of the day or as an appetizer.

MAKES 18

225g/8oz chicken breasts, skinned
2 tbsps oil
1 small onion, finely chopped
225g/8oz cooked potato, diced
1 tbsp red or green curry paste
2 tsps sugar
18 wonton wrappers
Oil for deep frying

Sweet and Sour Dipping Sauce
120g/4oz cucumber, finely chopped
120g/4oz carrots, finely chopped
140ml/¼ pint white wine vinegar
60g/2oz sugar
1 tsp chopped fresh coriander
Cucumber slices to garnish

1. Finely chop the chicken. Heat the oil in a wok and fry the onion and chicken for 3 minutes.

2. Stir in the potato, curry paste and sugar and fry for a few minutes.

3. Combine all the sauce ingredients in a bowl and stir until the sugar dissolves.

4. Lay the wonton wrappers out on a damp tea towel to prevent them drying out too quickly. Spoon a little of the filling into the centre of one of the wrappers.

5. Dampen the edges with water. Pull up the edges of the pastry and pinch together, enclosing the filling. Repeat until you have used up all the filling.

6. Heat the oil in a wok and deep fry a few at a time for 3-4 minutes or until crisp and golden.

7. Drain on kitchen paper. Serve with the sweet and sour dipping sauce. Garnish with cucumber slices.

TIME: Preparation takes 20 minutes and cooking takes 25-30 minutes.

BUYING GUIDE: Buy fresh or frozen wonton wrappers from Oriental supermarkets. Keep damp when using, to prevent them from drying out and becoming brittle.

PREPARATION: For method of preparation for curry paste, see recipe for Red Chicken Curry or Prawns in Green Curry Paste.

CHICKEN TIKKA

Chicken Tikka is one of the most popular chicken dishes cooked in the Tandoor, the Indian clay oven. This recipe is adapted to cook the chicken in the conventional oven at a high temperature.

SERVES 4

450g/1lb boneless, skinned chicken breast
1 tsp salt
Juice of ½ lemon
½ tsp tandoori colour or a few drops of red food colouring mixed with 1 tbsp tomato purée
2 cloves garlic, coarsely chopped
1.25cm/½-inch cube of fresh root ginger, peeled and coarsely chopped
2 tsps ground coriander
½ tsp ground allspice or garam masala
¼ of a whole nutmeg, finely grated
½ tsp ground turmeric
150g/5oz thick set natural yogurt
60ml/4 tbsps corn or vegetable oil
½ tsp chilli powder

1. Cut the chicken into 2.5cm/1-inch cubes. Sprinkle with ½ tsp of the salt, and the lemon juice – mix thoroughly, cover and keep aside for 30 minutes.

2. Put the rest of the ingredients into a food processor or liquidiser and blend until smooth.

3. Put this marinade into a sieve and hold the sieve over the chicken pieces. Press the marinade through the sieve with the back of a metal spoon until only a very coarse mixture is left.

4. Coat the chicken thoroughly with the sieved marinade, cover the container and leave to marinate for 6-8 hours or overnight in the refrigerator.

5. Preheat the oven to 230°C/450°F/Gas Mark 8.

6. Line a roasting tin with aluminium foil (this will help to maintain the high level of temperature required to cook the chicken quickly without drying it out).

7. Thread the chicken onto skewers, leaving 5mm/¼-inch gap between each piece (this is necessary for the heat to reach all sides of the chicken).

8. Place the skewers in the prepared roasting tin and brush with some of the remaining marinade.

9. Cook in the centre of the oven for 6-8 minutes.

10. Take the tin out of the oven, turn the skewers over and brush the pieces of chicken with the remaining marinade.

11. Return the tin to the oven and cook for a further 6-8 minutes.

12. Shake off any excess liquid from the chicken. (Strain the excess liquid and keep aside for Chicken Tikka Masala).

13. Place the skewers on a serving dish. You may take the tikka off the skewers if you wish, but allow the meat to cool slightly first.

TIME: Preparation takes 30-35 minutes plus at least 6 hours to marinate, cooking takes 15-18 minutes.

CHICKEN AND PEANUT CURRY

Sometimes known as dry chicken curry because of its thick sauce.

SERVES 4

450g/1lb chicken breasts, skinned and
    boned
Juice of 1 lemon
Juice of 1 lime
3 green chillies, seeded and chopped
60ml/4 tbsps oil
1 onion, chopped
¼ tsp ground cumin
¼ tsp ground coriander
120g/4oz ground roasted peanuts or
    crunchy peanut butter
140ml/¼ pint chicken stock
140ml/¼ pint thick coconut milk
90g/3oz freshly grated coconut flesh
1 tbsp sugar
1 tbsp fish sauce

1. Cut the chicken into bite-size pieces and place in a shallow dish. Mix together the lemon juice, lime juice and chopped chilli and pour over the chicken; toss until all the chicken is coated and leave to marinate for 1 hour.

2. Heat the oil in a wok and fry the onion until softened and beginning to brown. Stir in the cumin and coriander. Remove the chicken from the marinade and quickly fry until browned.

3. Add the marinade and cook over a high heat for 2-3 minutes.

4. Stir in the roasted peanuts, then gradually add the stock and coconut milk. Add the coconut flesh, sugar and fish sauce, simmer gently for 5 minutes or until the chicken is cooked.

TIME: Preparation takes 10 minutes plus 1 hour marinating and cooking
takes about 15 minutes.

BUYING GUIDE: Fish sauce is now available in some large supermarkets.

CHICKEN KORMA

Korma is a classic north Indian dish and there are many variations, some of which are quite elaborate. The recipe below, though simple and prepared with readily available ingredients, has all the characteristic features of this classic dish.

SERVES 4-6

2½lbs chicken joints, skin removed
2.5cm/1-inch cube of root ginger, finely grated
150g/5oz thick set natural yogurt
1 small onion, coarsely chopped
3-4 dried red chillies, coarsely chopped
2-4 cloves garlic, coarsely chopped
75ml/5 tbsps oil plus 2 tbsps extra oil
450g/1lb onions, finely sliced
1 tbsp ground coriander
½ tsp powdered black pepper
1 tsp garam masala
1 tsp ground turmeric
225ml/8 fl oz warm water (reduce quantity if using boneless chicken)
90g/3oz creamed coconut, cut into small pieces
1¼ tsps salt or to taste
2 heaped tbsps ground almonds
Juice of ½ lemon

---

1. Cut each chicken joint into half, separating leg from thigh and cutting each breast into two.

2. Mix with the ginger and yogurt, cover and leave to marinate in a cool place for 2-4 hours or in the refrigerator overnight.

3. Place the chopped onion, red chillies and garlic in a liquidiser or food processor and blend to a smooth paste. You may need to add a little water if you are using a liquidiser.

4. Heat the 75ml/5 tbsps oil over a medium heat and fry the sliced onions till they are golden brown. Remove the pan from the heat and using a slotted spoon, transfer the onions to another dish. Leave any oil in the pan.

5. Place the pan over a medium heat adding the extra 2 tbsps oil.

6. When hot, add the ground coriander, powdered pepper, garam masala and turmeric, stir rapidly (take the pan off the heat if the oil is too hot) and add the chicken along with the marinade. Adjust the heat to medium-high and fry the chicken for about 10 minutes, stirring frequently.

7. Add the liquidised spices and continue to fry for 6-8 minutes on a low heat.

8. Add the water and the coconut and bring to the boil. Stir until coconut is dissolved. Add fried onion slices and salt.

9. Reduce the heat to low, cover the pan and simmer for 25-30 minutes, or until the chicken is tender. Sprinkle the ground almonds over and mix well. Remove from the heat and add the lemon juice.

TIME: Preparation takes 15 minutes plus at least 2 hours to marinate, cooking takes 55 minutes.

SERVING IDEAS: Serve with Pilau Rice or raita.
Suitable for freezing.

CHICKEN WITH CHANNA DHAL

Channa dhal or dried chick peas have a distinctive flavour which goes particularly well with chicken. If these are unavailable use yellow split peas instead.

SERVES 6-8

225g/8oz channa dhal or yellow split peas
1kg/2¼lb chicken joints
2 tbsps cooking oil
2.5cm/1-inch cube of fresh root ginger, peeled and grated
3-4 cloves garlic, crushed
1 fresh green chilli, finely chopped

Make a paste of the following 6 ingredients by adding 60ml/2 fl oz water
1 tbsp ground coriander
1 tsp ground turmeric
½ tsp cayenne or chilli powder
½ tsp freshly ground black pepper
1 tsp ground cinnamon
½ tsp ground nutmeg

1¼ tsps salt or to taste
430ml/¾ pint warm water
45g/1½oz ghee or unsalted butter
1 large onion, finely sliced
2 tbsps chopped coriander leaves
1 medium-sized ripe tomato, sliced

1. Clean and wash the channa dhal or the split peas and soak them in plenty of cold water for about 2 hours. Drain well.

2. Cut each chicken joint into two, separating leg from thigh. Wash and pat dry.

3. In a heavy-based pan, heat the oil gently over a low heat and fry the ginger, garlic and green chilli for 1 minute.

4. Add the spice paste, stir and fry for 2-3 minutes.

5. Add the chicken, adjust the heat to medium-high, stir and fry the chicken for 3-4 minutes until it changes colour.

6. Add the dhal or split peas, stir and fry for a further 3-4 minutes.

7. Stir in the salt and add the water. Bring to the boil, cover the pan and simmer for 35-40 minutes, or until the chicken and the dhal are tender.

8. Meanwhile, in a separate pan, melt the ghee or butter over a medium heat and fry the onions for 8-10 minutes, stirring frequently, until they are golden brown.

9. Add the onion to the chicken along with any remaining ghee in the pan. Add half the coriander leaves and stir until all the ingredients are mixed thoroughly. Cover the pan and simmer for 10 minutes.

10. Put the chicken in a serving dish and garnish with the tomato and the remaining coriander leaves.

TIME: Preparation takes 25 minutes plus 2 hours needed to soak the dhal, cooking takes 55 minutes.

MURGHI AUR ALOO

This recipe is a fine example of the Persian influence in Indian cookery. Chicken and potatoes are cooked with saffron and a generous amount of fresh coriander.

SERVES 4-6

1kg/2¼lbs chicken joints, skinned
1½ tsps salt or to taste
2.5cm/1-inch cube of fresh root ginger, peeled and coarsely chopped
4-6 cloves garlic, coarsely chopped

Grind the following 6 ingredients in a coffee grinder
2 tsps cumin seeds
4-6 dried red chillies
Seeds of 2 black cardamoms; or 4 whole green cardamoms
6 whole cloves
2 cinnamon sticks, broken into 2-3 pieces
6 black peppercorns

Grind the following 2 ingredients separately
1 tbsp white poppy seeds
10 raw whole cashews

60ml/4 tbsps cold water
60g/2oz ghee or unsalted butter
30g/1oz fresh coriander leaves and stalks, finely chopped
1-2 fresh green chillies, halved lengthwise; seeded for a milder flavour
½ tsp ground turmeric
280ml/½ pint warm water
½ tsp saffron strands
450g/1lb medium potatoes, peeled and quartered
150g/5oz soured cream
2-3 hard-boiled eggs, quartered lengthwise

1. Cut each chicken joint into two; separate leg from thigh and cut each breast into two pieces.

2. Add the salt to the ginger and garlic and crush them to a pulp.

3. Convert the ground ingredients, including the poppy seeds and the cashews, to a thick paste by adding the cold water. Break up any lumps with the back of a spoon.

4. Melt the ghee or butter over a low heat and add the ginger/garlic paste. Cook for 2-3 minutes stirring continuously.

5. Add the spice paste, stir and fry for 2-3 minutes.

6. Add chicken and cook for 5-6 minutes, over a medium-high heat, until it browns.

7. Add the coriander leaves, green chillies and turmeric, stir and fry for a further 2-3 minutes.

8. Add the warm water, bring to the boil and add the saffron strands. Cover and simmer for 15 minutes.

9. Add the potatoes and cook for a further 20 minutes or until the chicken and the potatoes are tender and the sauce is fairly thick.

10. Beat the soured cream until smooth and stir into the chicken. Cook uncovered for 6-8 minutes stirring frequently. Remove from the heat.

11. Arrange the chicken curry in a serving dish and garnish with the quarters of hard-boiled eggs.

DAHI MURGHI

Dahi Murghi or chicken in yogurt needs little effort to cook and is simply gorgeous. The chicken is marinated in a yogurt-laced mixture and simmered until tender. Its simple method of cooking means that it can easily be fitted into a busy life style.

SERVES 4-6

1kg/2¼lbs chicken joints, skinned
150g/5oz carton of thick set natural yogurt
3-4 cloves garlic, coarsely chopped
2.5cm/1-inch cube of root ginger, peeled and coarsely chopped
2-3 dried red chillies
½ tsp ground turmeric
1 tbsp ground coriander
60ml/4 tbsps cooking oil
1 large onion, finely sliced
2-4 fresh green chillies, whole
1 tsp salt
½ tsp garam masala
2 tbsps chopped coriander leaves

1. Cut each chicken joint into two, separate leg from thigh and cut each breast into two pieces.

2. Put the yogurt, garlic, ginger, dried red chillies, turmeric and ground coriander in a liquidiser and blend until smooth.

3. Put the chicken in a large bowl and pour the marinade over. Mix thoroughly, cover, and leave to marinate for 6-8 hours or overnight, in the refrigerator.

4. Put the chicken into a heavy-based pan with a lid and place over a medium heat, stirring occasionally, until the chicken is heated through. Cover the pan and simmer gently for 25-30 minutes, or until the chicken is tender. Remove the pan from the heat.

5. Meanwhile heat the oil over a medium heat in a large frying pan and brown the onion.

6. Add the chicken and cook uncovered for 5-6 minutes stirring frequently.

7. Add the whole green chillies, salt and garam masala and cook for a further 3-4 minutes.

8. Remove the pan from the heat and stir in half the coriander leaves.

9. Put the chicken into a heated serving dish and sprinkle the remaining coriander leaves on top.

TIME: Preparation takes 15 minutes plus at least 6 hours to marinate, cooking takes 45-50 minutes.

JAVANESE CURRY

*This Javanese chicken curry contains a wonderful combination of flavours –
aubergine, lemon grass, coconut milk, cinnamon and ginger.*

SERVES 4

1 aubergine
2 tbsps oil
2 medium onions, finely chopped
6 cloves garlic, crushed
1 × 1.4kg/3lb chicken, cut into 8 pieces
1 small piece fresh root ginger, chopped
2 tsps chilli powder
1 tsp ground coriander
½ tsp ground turmeric
570ml/1 pint coconut milk
2 whole cloves
1 small piece cinnamon stick
1 stalk lemon grass, peeled and the core
    chopped
1 tbsp lime juice
Salt

Garnish

60g/2oz chopped almonds or macadamia
    nuts
22g/4 tbsps desiccated coconut

1. Slice aubergine in half and score the cut surface of each half. Sprinkle with salt and stand for 30 minutes. Rinse, dry and cube.

2. Heat a large frying pan or wok and add the oil. When hot, add the onion and garlic and fry until lightly brown.

3. Lower the heat and add the chicken and aubergine. Cook until the chicken is lightly browned.

4. Add the ginger, chilli powder, coriander, and turmeric, and cook for 1 minute.

5. Gradually pour on the coconut milk and stir well. Add the cloves, cinnamon stick and lemon grass.

6. Bring to the boil, reduce the heat and allow to simmer very gently for about 50 minutes or until the chicken is tender.

7. When the chicken is cooked add the lime juice and season with salt to taste.

8. Serve garnished with chopped almonds or macadamia nuts and desiccated coconut.

TIME: Preparation takes 40 minutes including standing time for the aubergine; cooking takes about 50 minutes.

WATCHPOINT: Do not soak the aubergine for more than 30 minutes else it will become too dehydrated.

CHICKEN DHANSAK

Dhansak is a combination of two or three types of lentils and meat or chicken.

SERVES 6-8

1kg/2¼lbs chicken joints, skinned
1 tsp salt or to taste
2.5cm/1-inch cube of fresh root ginger,
    peeled and coarsely chopped
4-6 cloves garlic, chopped

*Grind the following 10 ingredients in a
coffee grinder*
1 tsp coriander seeds
1 tsp cumin seeds
1 tsp fennel seeds
4 green cardamoms
5cm/2 inches cinnamon stick, broken
4-6 dried red chillies
10 black peppercorns
2 bay leaves
¼ tsp fenugreek seeds
½ tsp black mustard seeds

2 tbsps ghee or unsalted butter
120ml/4 fl oz warm water

For the dhal
90g/3oz toor dhal (yellow split peas)
90g/3oz masoor dhal (red split lentils)
75ml/5 tbsps cooking oil
1 large onion, finely chopped
1 tsp ground turmeric
1 tsp garam masala
570ml/1 pint warm water
1 tsp salt or to taste
1 tsp tamarind concentrate (available from
    Indian grocers) or 1½ tbsps lemon juice
1 tbsp chopped coriander leaves, optional

1. Cut each chicken portion into two.

2. Add the salt to the ginger and garlic and crush to a pulp.

3. Make a paste of the ground ingredients and the ginger/garlic pulp by adding 6 tbsps water. Pour this mixture over the chicken and mix to coat thoroughly. Cover and set aside for 4-6 hours or overnight in the refrigerator.

4. Melt the ghee and fry the chicken for 6-8 minutes, stirring often. Add the water, bring to the boil, cover and simmer for 20 minutes. Stir several times.

5. Meanwhile, mix together the toor and masoor dhals, wash and drain well.

6. Heat the oil and fry the onions for 5 minutes, stirring often. Add the turmeric and garam masala, stir and fry for 1 minute. Add the dhal, and fry gently for 5 minutes, stirring often. Add the water and salt, bring to the boil, cover and simmer for 30 minutes until soft, stirring occasionally. Remove from the heat.

7. Using a metal spoon, push the cooked dhal, a little at a time, through a sieve until there is only a very dry and coarse mixture left to discard.

8. Pour the sieved dhal over the chicken, cover and bring to the boil, then simmer for 20-25 minutes. Stir occasionally at first, but more frequently during the latter half of cooking, to ensure that the mixture does not stick.

9. Dissolve the tamarind pulp in 3 tbsps boiling water. Add this to the chicken, stir and mix thoroughly. Cover and simmer for 5 minutes. Stir in the coriander leaves and lemon juice if using, and remove from heat.

RED CHICKEN CURRY

Red and green curry pastes are the basis of most Thai curries and this is a simple one using red curry paste.

SERVES 4

Red Curry Paste

1 small onion, finely chopped

3 cloves garlic, crushed

10 small red chillies, chopped

1 tsp grated fresh root ginger

1 stem lemon grass, chopped

2 tsps chopped fresh coriander, stems and root

Large pinch cumin

1 tsp shrimp paste

2 tbsps oil

Curry

450g/1lb chicken breasts, skinned and boned

2 tbsps oil

2 onions, cut into wedges

3 tbsps red curry paste

2 Kaffir lime leaves, shredded

280ml/½ pint thick coconut milk

120g/4oz canned sliced bamboo shoots (drained weight)

1 tbsp fish sauce

2 tbsps sugar

1. Make the curry paste by placing all the ingredients in a food processor and grinding to a paste. Store in a small jar in the refrigerator until required.

2. Cut the chicken into bite-size pieces. Heat the oil and fry the onion and chicken for 5 minutes or until the onion is softened and beginning to brown. Remove from the pan and set aside.

3. Add the 3 tbsp curry paste and lime leaves to the pan and fry for a few minutes. Stir in half of the coconut milk and boil rapidly for 3 minutes.

4. Return the chicken to the wok and add the bamboo shoots, fish sauce and sugar. Simmer gently for 5 minutes or until the chicken is cooked.

5. Stir in the remaining coconut milk and cook until heated through.

TIME: Preparation takes 15 minutes and cooking takes 15 minutes.

COOK'S TIP: The curry paste will keep for 1 month in the refrigerator.

PREPARATION: To use lemon grass, remove the dried tough outer leaves and finely chop the soft inner core.

MILD FRUITY CHICKEN CURRY

This mild fruity chicken curry is wonderfully creamy and tastes delicious.

SERVES 4

140ml/¼ pint boiling water
140ml/¼ pint milk
120g/4oz desiccated coconut
60ml/4 tbsps oil
4 chicken joints, skinned
2 tbsps curry powder
30g/1oz flour
280ml/½ pint chicken stock
400g/14oz can pineapple chunks
1 tbsp onion flakes
1 tsp salt
2 tbsps single cream

1. Mix together the boiling water and milk in a bowl. Stir in the coconut and leave to infuse for about 2 hours. Strain liquid and discard the coconut.

2. Heat half the oil in a large, heavy based saucepan. Add the chicken pieces and fry until golden brown on all sides. Remove the chicken pieces from the pan with a slotted spoon.

3. Heat the remaining oil in the pan. Stir the curry powder into the oil and fry for about ½ minute.

4. Remove the pan from the heat and stir in the flour. Gradually stir in the stock, the strained coconut milk, the juice from the tin of pineapple and the onion flakes.

5. Return the chicken to the pan with the salt. Bring to the boil, stirring occasionally.

6. Cover and simmer for 1 hour, stirring occasionally.

7. Stir in the pineapple chunks and heat through, then remove from the heat and stir in the cream.

8. Taste and adjust the seasoning if necessary and serve immediately.

TIME: Preparation takes 10 minutes, plus 2 hours soaking time for coconut; cooking takes 1 hour.

COOK'S TIP: Use 280ml/½ pint canned coconut milk for quickness instead of soaking the desiccated.

COCONUT CURRIED CHICKEN

This blend of spices mixed with chicken, coconut milk and sweet potatoes makes a delicious combination.

SERVES 4

3 tbsps oil
1 tsp curry powder
1 tsp ground coriander
½ tsp ground cumin
¼ tsp ground cinnamon
1 tsp grated fresh root ginger
1 clove garlic, crushed
1 medium onion, finely chopped
1.4kg/3lbs chicken pieces, skinned
2 curry leaves or bay leaves
570ml/1 pint coconut milk
1 tbsp lime juice
225g/8oz sweet potatoes, peeled and cubed
Salt and pepper
Desiccated coconut

1. Heat the oil in a heavy-based frying pan or wok and cook all the spices for 1 minute.

2. Add the garlic, ginger and onion and cook over a gentle heat until the onion is softened.

3. Add the chicken pieces and stir into the spice mixture to coat them thoroughly.

4. Add the curry leaves or bay leaves and pour on the coconut milk and lime juice.

5. Add sweet potatoes and salt and pepper to taste, then bring the mixture gently to the boil.

6. Reduce the heat and allow to simmer for about 45-50 minutes or until the chicken is tender and the sauce is thickened.

7. Adjust the seasoning and sprinkle with desiccated coconut to serve.

TIME: Preparation takes 20 minutes, and cooking takes about 50-55 minutes.

BUYING GUIDE: Canned or instant coconut milk is now available in many ordinary supermarkets as well as specialist Oriental stores.

MURGHI BADAMI

Murghi Badami is a richer version of Chicken Korma, where the chicken is cooked entirely in natural yogurt and single cream. No water is added to the chicken and the result is a thick and silky gravy with a delightful taste.

SERVES 4-6

1kg/2¼lbs chicken joints, skinned

1 tsp salt or to taste

2.5cm/1-inch cube of root ginger, peeled and chopped

3-4 cloves garlic, chopped

1 tsp freshly ground black pepper

1 tbsp lemon juice

280g/10oz thick set natural yogurt

60g/2oz ghee or unsalted butter

2 medium onions, finely sliced

6 green cardamoms, split open the top of each pod

1 tbsp ground coriander

1 tsp ground turmeric

150ml/5 fl oz single cream

¼-½ tsp chilli powder

60g/2oz flaked almonds

1 heaped tbsp ground almonds

1. Cut each chicken joint into two – separating leg from thigh and cutting each breast into two pieces. Wash the chicken and dry with a cloth or kitchen paper. Make small incisions on both sides of the pieces of chicken with a sharp knife. This is to allow the spices to penetrate deep inside.

2. Add the salt to the ginger and garlic and crush to a fine pulp. Mix with the pepper and lemon juice. Rub this mixture into the chicken, cover it and keep aside for ½-1 hour.

3. Beat the yogurt until smooth and keep aside.

4. Melt the ghee or butter over a medium heat and fry the onions for 10-12 minutes, until well browned. Remove pan from the heat and squeeze out the excess fat by pressing the onions to the side of the pan. Transfer the onions to a plate.

5. Return the pan to heat and add cardamoms and coriander, stir and fry for 30 seconds. Add the chicken, and fry over a medium-high heat for 5-6 minutes, stirring continuously.

6. Stir in the turmeric and the yogurt and simmer; cover the pan and cook for 15 minutes, stirring occasionally.

7. Reserve 2 tbsps of the fried onions and add the rest to the chicken along with the cream, chilli powder and the almonds, stir and mix well. Cover and simmer for a further 15-20 minutes stirring occasionally.

8. Sprinkle the ground almonds over, and mix well, cover and simmer for 6-8 minutes. Remove from the heat.

9. Put the chicken in a serving dish and garnish with the remaining fried onions.

TIME: Preparation takes 25-30 minutes plus time needed for marinating, cooking takes 55-60 minutes.

SERVING IDEAS: Serve with any Indian bread or Pilau Rice.

MURGHI JHAL FREZI

This delicious and relatively easy dish to cook, with thick spice paste clinging to the pieces of chicken, makes it an irresistible choice for entertaining.

SERVES 4-6

1kg/2¼lbs chicken joints
3 large onions, finely chopped
175ml/6 fl oz water
2.5cm/1-inch cube of root ginger, peeled and grated
2-4 cloves garlic, crushed
1 tsp ground coriander
1 tsp ground cumin
1 tsp ground ajwain or caraway
½ tsp ground turmeric
½ chilli powder
2 cinnamon sticks, 5cm/2-inch long each, broken up
2 black cardamoms, split open at the top of each pod
4 whole cloves
75ml/5 tbsps cooking oil
1¼ tsps salt or to taste
1 tbsp tomato purée
1-2 fresh green chillies, sliced lengthwise; seeded for a milder flavour
2 tbsps chopped coriander leaves

1. Skin and cut each joint into two, separate leg from thigh and cut each breast into two pieces, wash and dry on kitchen paper.

2. Put the chicken in a saucepan, add half the chopped onions, the water, ginger, garlic, coriander, cumin, ajwain, turmeric, chilli powder, cinnamon, cardamom and cloves. Bring to the boil, stir and mix thoroughly. Cover and simmer for 20-25 minutes.

3. In a separate pan, heat the oil over a medium heat and fry the rest of the onions until they are golden brown.

4. Remove each piece of chicken with a pair of tongs and add to the onions. Fry over a medium heat for about 5 minutes until the chicken is brown.

5. Now add half the spiced liquid in which the chicken was cooked, stir and fry for 4-5 minutes. Add the rest of the liquid and fry for a further 4-5 minutes.

6. Add salt, tomato purée, green chillies and coriander leaves, stir and fry on a low heat for 5-6 minutes. Remove from the heat and serve.

TIME: Preparation takes 20-25 minutes, cooking takes 45-50 minutes.

VARIATION: Use lean pork instead of chicken.

WATCHPOINT: Reduce the cooking time for boneless chicken and in stage 5, fry the chicken for a little longer to reach the paste-like consistency required.

CHICKEN TIKKA MASALA

The delicate flavour of chicken smothered in almond and cream sauce makes this a wonderful choice for a dinner party or a special occasion menu.

SERVES 4

450g/1lb Chicken Tikka (see separate recipe)
1.25cm/½-inch cube of root ginger, peeled and coarsely chopped
2 cloves garlic, coarsely chopped
1 tsp salt or to taste
60g/2oz unsalted butter
1 small onion, finely chopped
¼ tsp ground turmeric
½ tsp ground cumin
½ tsp ground coriander
½ tsp garam masala
¼-½ tsp chilli powder
120ml/4 fl oz liquid, made up of the reserved juice from the precooked Chicken Tikka and warm water
280ml/½ pint double cream
2 heaped tbsps ground almonds

1. Mix together the ginger, garlic and ½ tsp of the salt and crush to a pulp. Keep the remaining salt aside for later use.

2. Melt the butter gently and fry the onion for 2-3 minutes.

3. Add the ginger/garlic paste and cook for 1 minute.

4. Stir in the turmeric and then the cumin, coriander, garam masala and chilli powder. Stir and cook for 2 minutes.

5. Add the liquid and stir gently.

6. Gradually add the cream and stir.

7. Add the remaining salt and simmer for 5 minutes and then add the chicken. Adjust the heat to low, cover and cook for 10 minutes.

8. Stir in the ground almonds and simmer for 5-6 minutes.

9. Remove from heat.

TIME: Preparation takes 10 minutes plus time needed to marinate the tikka, cooking takes 25 minutes plus time needed to cook the tikka.

SERVING IDEAS: Serve with rice.

CHICKEN DO-PIAZA

A fairly easy dish to prepare in which more than the usual quantity of onions are used. The name itself suggests the quantity of onions required, Do means twice and Piaz means onion. The literal translation would, therefore, be 'chicken with twice the amount of onions'.

SERVES 4-6

1.2kg/2½lbs chicken joints, skin removed

1 large onion, coarsely chopped

2.5cm/1-inch cube of root ginger, peeled and coarsely chopped

3-4 cloves garlic, coarsely chopped

60ml/4 tbsps cooking oil

1 tsp ground turmeric

1 tsp ground coriander

1 tsp ground cumin

¼-½ tsp chilli powder

1 small can of tomatoes

175ml/6 fl oz warm water

2 cinnamon sticks, each 5cm/2-inches long; broken up

4 green cardamoms; split open at the top of each pod

4 whole cloves

2 dried bay leaves, crumbled

1¼ tsps salt or to taste

2 level tbsps ghee or unsalted butter

1 large onion, finely sliced

1 tbsp chopped coriander leaves (optional)

1. Cut each chicken breast into 3 pieces. If you are using legs, separate from thigh. Wash and dry on kitchen paper.

2. Place the chopped onion, ginger and garlic into a liquidiser or food processor and liquidise to a smooth paste, add a little water, if necessary, to facilitate blade movement.

3. Heat the oil over a medium heat and add the liquidised ingredients. Stir and fry for 4-5 minutes.

4. Add the turmeric, coriander, cumin and chilli powder. Fry for 4-5 minutes stirring frequently, adding 1 tbsp juice, from the can of tomatoes, at a time to prevent the spices from sticking to the pan. When you have used up all the tomato juice, add the chicken and fry it over medium-high heat until the chicken has changed colour.

5. Add the water, cinnamon, cardamom, cloves, bay leaves, salt and the tomatoes. Bring to the boil, cover and simmer for about 25 minutes until the chicken is tender and the sauce is fairly thick. Cook uncovered, if necessary, to thicken the sauce.

6. Heat the ghee or butter and fry the sliced onion for 5 minutes. Add the onions along with the ghee to the chicken. Remove from the heat and stir in the coriander leaves.

TIME: Preparation takes 15 minutes, cooking takes 45 minutes.

SERVING IDEAS: Serve with Naan bread and a raita or with Plain Boiled Rice and New Potato Fry.
Suitable for freezing.

Sabji Masala Murghi

This chicken dish is wonderful when time may be short to cook a separate vegetable dish, because a selection of vegetables are added to the chicken at different stages. Frozen vegetables are used in this recipe; if fresh vegetables are used, the cooking time should be adjusted accordingly.

SERVES 4-6

1kg/2¼lbs chicken leg portions
200ml/7 fl oz water
90g/3oz roasted cashews
60g/2oz ghee or unsalted butter
2.5cm/1-inch cube of root ginger, peeled and finely grated
4-6 cloves garlic, finely chopped

Grind the following 4 ingredients in a coffee grinder
¼ tsp ground nutmeg
6 whole green cardamoms
1 tsp caraway seeds
4-6 dried red chillies

1¼ tsps salt or to taste
60g/2oz whole baby carrots
60g/2oz frozen garden peas
60g/2oz frozen sweetcorn
4 spring onions, coarsely chopped
1 small green pepper, finely shredded

1. Skin the chicken and separate legs from thighs; wash and pat dry.

2. Put 120ml/4 fl oz of the water into a blender, add the cashews, and blend to a smooth paste.

3. Melt the ghee or butter over a medium heat and fry the ginger and garlic for 1 minute.

4. Adjust the heat to low and add the ground ingredients, stir and fry for 1 minute.

5. Add the chicken, adjust the heat to medium-high and fry the chicken for 5-6 minutes until it changes colour.

6. Add the cashew paste, stir and mix thoroughly. Rinse out the blender container with the remaining water and add to the chicken.

7. Add the salt, mix well, cover the pan and cook over low heat for 15 minutes, stirring occasionally.

8. Add the carrots, stir and mix; cover and cook for a further 15 minutes.

9. Add the peas and the sweetcorn, mix well, cover the pan and cook over a medium heat for 5 minutes.

10. Reserve half the spring onions and add the rest to the chicken along with the green pepper. Cook, uncovered, for 5-6 minutes, stirring frequently. Remove from the heat.

11. Put the chicken in a serving dish and garnish with the reserved spring onions.

TIME: Preparation takes 20-25 minutes, cooking takes 45-50 minutes.

SERVING IDEAS: Serve with plain fried rice.

CHICKEN TOMATO

Chicken cooked in a spicy tomato sauce makes an interesting alternative to an ordinary casserole.

SERVES 4

1 onion, chopped
45ml/3 tbsps oil or 45g/1½oz ghee
2.5cm/1-inch cinnamon stick
1 bayleaf
6 cloves
6 green cardamoms
2.5cm/1-inch fresh root ginger, peeled and sliced
4 cloves garlic, chopped
1 × 1.4kg/3lb chicken cut into 8-10 pieces
1 tsp chilli powder
1 tsp ground cumin
1 tsp ground coriander
400g/14oz can tomatoes, crushed
1 tsp salt
2 sprigs fresh coriander leaves, chopped
2 green chillies, halved

1. Sauté the onion for 2 minutes in oil or ghee, to soften.

2. Add the cinnamon, bayleaf, cloves, cardamoms and cook for 1 minute, then add ginger and garlic and fry for 30 seconds.

3. Add chicken pieces and sprinkle with the chilli powder, cumin and coriander. Fry for 2-3 minutes, then add the crushed tomatoes.

4. Season with salt and add the fresh coriander and chillies.

5. Stir the chicken to mix well. Cover and cook for 40-45 minutes or until chicken is tender.

TIME: Preparation takes about 30 minutes and cooking takes 40-45 minutes.

COOK'S TIP: Remove chilli seeds if a more subtle flavour is required.

SERVING IDEAS: Accompany with Plain Boiled Rice and poppadoms.

CHICKEN CURRY (MILD)

This mild curry is typical of northern India and has a lovely creamy sauce.

SERVES 4

1.4kg/3lbs chicken pieces
1 tbsp peanut oil
1 onion, finely chopped
2 cloves garlic, crushed
½ tsp grated ginger
2 tsps curry powder
½ tsp salt
1 tbsp vinegar
140ml/¼ pint coconut cream
140ml/¼ pint milk

1. Cut the chicken into smaller pieces: breast-meat into 4 pieces, thigh-meat into 2 pieces, and wings separated at joints.

2. Heat the oil until hot. Reduce the heat. Add the onion, garlic and ginger and cook gently, stirring continuously. Cook for 10 minutes, or until the onion is soft and golden brown.

3. Increase the heat and add the curry powder. Fry for 30 seconds. Add the salt and vinegar, and cook for 1 minute.

4. Add the chicken, and turn so that mixture coats the chicken well.

5. Add the coconut cream and milk, and simmer gently over a low heat for 20 minutes.

TIME: Preparation takes 10 minutes and cooking takes about 30 minutes.

SERVING IDEAS: Serve with Pilau Rice and poppadoms.

COOK'S TIP: Instant, powdered coconut milk can be used to replace the coconut cream and is a good item to keep in your store cupboard.

MUSSAMAN CURRY

This curry illustrates the Indian influence on some of Thailand's cuisine.

SERVES 4

4 cardamom pods
½ tsp coriander seeds
½ tsp caraway seeds
2 whole cloves
5 small red chillies, chopped
1 clove garlic, crushed
1 stem lemon grass, roughly chopped
2 spring onions, chopped
½ tsp grated fresh root ginger
¼ tsp ground nutmeg
1 tbsp oil
Oil for shallow frying
340g/12oz potatoes, peeled and cut into
    chunks
2-3 onions, cut into wedges
675g/1½lb sirloin steak, cut into 2.5cm/
    1-inch cubes
430ml/¾ pint thin coconut milk
2 tbsps dark brown sugar
1 tsp tamarind juice

Chopped coriander to garnish

1. Crush the cardamom pods with the side of a knife and remove the seeds.

2. Place the coriander seeds, caraway seeds, cardamom and cloves in a wok and dry-fry for 1 minute, tossing frequently to prevent burning. Remove from the heat.

3. Mix the fried seeds with the chillies, garlic, lemon grass, spring onion, ginger, nutmeg and oil. Pound together in a pestle and mortar to a paste.

4. Heat the oil for shallow frying in the wok and fry the potato and onion wedges for 5 minutes or until they begin to soften, then remove and set aside.

5. Add the meat to the pan and fry until browned. Stir in a quarter of the coconut milk and simmer gently for 30 minutes or until the meat is tender.

6. Remove the meat from the pan with a slotted spoon and set aside. Add the chilli mixture to the pan and boil rapidly for 5 minutes, then blend in the remaining coconut milk.

7. Return the meat, onions and potatoes to the wok. Stir in the sugar and tamarind juice. Cook gently for 20 minutes. Garnish with chopped coriander.

TIME: Preparation takes 25 minutes and cooking takes about 1 hour.

PREPARATION: To extract tamarind juice, soak 1 tbsp compressed pulp in 4 tbsp warm water for 5 minutes. Squeeze and knead the tamarind to dissolve it then strain out the seeds or fibre.

COOK'S TIP: To use lemon grass, remove the dried outer tough leaves and chop the soft inner core.

ROGAN JOSH

Rogan Josh finds its origin in Kashmir, the northern-most state in India. In the recipe below, more than the usual quantity of spices are used, but these are toned down by using a large quantity of tomatoes and a little double cream.

SERVES 4-6

3 tbsps ghee or unsalted butter

1kg/2¼lbs leg of lamb, without bones, cut into 4cm/1½-inch cubes

1 tbsp ground cumin

1 tbsp ground coriander

1 tsp ground turmeric

1 tsp chilli powder

2.5cm/1-inch cube of root ginger, peeled and grated

2-4 cloves garlic, crushed

225-275g/8-10oz onions, finely sliced

1 × 400g/14oz can of tomatoes, chopped or whole

1 tbsp tomato purée

120ml/4 fl oz warm water

1¼ tsps salt or to taste

90ml/3 fl oz double cream

2 tsps garam masala

2 tbsps chopped coriander leaves

1. Melt 2 tbsps of the ghee or butter over a medium heat and lightly brown the meat in 2-3 batches. Remove each batch with a slotted spoon and keep aside.

2. Lower the heat to minimum and add the cumin, coriander, turmeric, chilli powder, ginger and garlic. Stir and fry for 30 seconds.

3. Adjust the heat to medium and add the meat along with all the juices in the container. Stir and fry for 3-4 minutes and add the onions. Fry for 5-6 minutes stirring frequently.

4. Now add the tomatoes and tomato purée – stir and cook for 2-3 minutes.

5. Add the water and salt, bring to the boil, cover and simmer for about 60 minutes, or until the meat is tender.

6. Stir in the cream and remove from the heat.

7. In a separate pan melt the remaining ghee over a medium heat and add the garam masala, stir briskly and add to the meat.

8. Transfer a little meat gravy to the pan in which the garam masala was fried – stir thoroughly to ensure that any remaining garam masala and ghee mixture is fully incorporated into the gravy and add this to the meat. Mix well.

9. Stir in the coriander leaves.

TIME: Preparation takes 20 minutes, cooking takes 1 hour 30 minutes.

SERVING IDEAS: Serve with Plain Boiled Rice or plain fried rice. If you are entertaining, add naan bread and a raita.

TO FREEZE: Freeze before adding the cream, garam masala and coriander leaves. Defrost thoroughly before reheating. Bring to the boil, cook for 10 minutes, add the cream and remove from heat. Add garam masala and coriander leaves.

MEAT DILRUBA

This delicious meat curry is in a class of its own. It is cooked in two stages making it easier to get much of the preparation and cooking out of the way in advance.

SERVES 4-6

1kg/2¼lbs boned leg of lamb

1.25cm/½-inch cube of root ginger, peeled and finely chopped

3-4 cloves garlic, finely chopped

1¼ tsps salt or to taste

1 tsp ground turmeric

150g/5oz thick set natural yogurt

1 large onion, finely sliced

3-4 dried red chillies, coarsely chopped

150ml/5 fl oz water

2 tbsps ghee or unsalted butter

2 tbsps ground coriander

Grind together in a coffee grinder

1 tbsp white poppy seeds

1 tsp fenugreek seeds

60g/2oz desiccated coconut, grind separately in a coffee grinder, about 15g/ ½oz at a time

150ml/5 fl oz milk

15g/½oz finely chopped coriander leaves

1 fresh green chilli, cut lengthwise into thin strips; remove seeds if preferred

1. Trim off excess fat from the meat, pat dry, and cut into 2.5cm/1-inch cubes.

2. Put the ginger, garlic and salt in a pestle and mortar and crush them to a pulp. Alternatively, use a chopping board and crush them with the end of a wooden rolling pin.

3. Mix together the ginger/garlic pulp, turmeric and the yogurt and beat until the yogurt is smooth. Add this to the meat, mix thoroughly, cover the container and leave to marinate for 4-6 hours or overnight in the refrigerator.

4. Put the marinated meat into a heavy-based saucepan, add the onions, red chillies and the water. Bring to a slow simmer over a gentle heat. Cover the pan and simmer for 50-60 minutes or until the meat is tender. Remove from the heat.

5. Melt the ghee over a medium heat and add the ground coriander, stir and fry for 30 seconds. Add the ground poppy and fenugreek seeds and fry for 1-2 minutes, stirring constantly, until the mixture is lightly browned.

6. Lift the meat out with a slotted spoon and add to the poppy/fenugreek mixture. Stir and fry over medium-high heat for 6-7 minutes, until all the moisture evaporates. Add the ground coconut, stir and fry for 2 minutes. Now add the milk and the liquid in which the meat was cooked. Stir and mix thoroughly. Cook, uncovered, over a low heat for 4-5 minutes, stirring frequently.

7. Stir in the coriander leaves and the green chilli and remove from the heat.

TIME: Preparation takes 25-30 minutes plus at least 4 hours for marinating, cooking takes 1 hour 15 minutes.

GOAN CURRY

This dish includes curry leaves, which are used extensively in southern Indian cooking. It is one of the main ingredients in commercially prepared curry powder.

SERVES 3-4

60g/2oz ghee or 3 tbsps oil
1 large onion, chopped
1 bayleaf
2.5cm/1-inch cinnamon stick
5 green cardamoms
6 cloves
1½ tsps garlic paste
1 tsp ginger paste
8 curry leaves
450g/1lb lean pork, cut into cubes
1 tbsp tamarind pulp
140ml/¼ pint natural yogurt
¼ tsp turmeric powder
1 tsp ground black pepper
1 tsp ground cumin
1 tsp ground coriander
½ tsp sugar
1 tbsp desiccated coconut
Salt to taste
140ml/¼ pint water
2 sprigs fresh coriander, chopped
2 green chillies, chopped

1. Heat the ghee or oil and fry the onion until golden brown.

2. Add the bayleaf, cinnamon, cardamoms, cloves, garlic, ginger and curry leaves and fry for 1-2 minutes.

3. Add the pork and fry for 5-7 minutes or until the liquid from the pork has evaporated.

4. Add the tamarind pulp, yogurt, turmeric, black pepper, cumin, coriander, sugar, coconut and salt to taste.

5. Mix well, cover and cook for 20-30 minutes.

6. Add the water if the mixture is too dry, and stir in the fresh coriander and chillies.

7. Cover and cook for 20-25 minutes or until pork is tender. The dish should have a smooth gravy.

TIME: Preparation takes about 20 minutes and cooking takes about 1 hour.

BUYING GUIDE: Curry leaves, available from Asian supermarkets are sold dried – these can be stored in a jar – or fresh, in which case they can be frozen and used straight from the freezer.

KOFTA BHOONA

Kofta Bhoona consists of tiny meatballs the size of marbles which are coated with a delicious spice paste.

SERVES 4-6

450g/1lb fine lean mince, lamb or beef
1 large clove of garlic, crushed
1 tsp garam masala
1-2 fresh green chillies, seeded and minced
1½ tsps salt or to taste
2 tbsps fresh coriander leaves, minced
3 tbsps cooking oil
1 large onion, finely chopped
5mm/¼-inch cube of root ginger, peeled
    and grated
2 tsps ground coriander
1 tsp ground cumin

Make a paste of the following 5 ingredients
½-1 tsp chilli powder
2 cloves garlic, crushed
½ tsp ground turmeric
2 tbsps tomato purée
120ml/4 fl oz cold water

225ml/8 fl oz warm water
60g/2oz frozen garden peas
¼ tsp garam masala
2 tbsps chopped coriander leaves

1. Put the mince in a large bowl and add the garlic, garam masala, green chillies, 1 tsp of the salt and the coriander leaves. Mix thoroughly and knead the mince until it is smooth.

2. Divide the mixture into about 28-30 balls (koftas). Make the koftas by rolling the balls between the palms in a circular motion until they are smooth and round.

3. Heat the oil over a medium heat, preferably in a nonstick or cast iron pan, and fry the koftas in 2-3 batches. Turn the koftas as they brown and when they are brown all over, remove with a slotted spoon and drain on kitchen paper.

4. In the same oil, fry the onions and ginger for 6-8 minutes, stirring frequently, until the onions are golden brown.

5. Add the ground coriander, stir and fry over a low heat for 30 seconds. Now add the ground cumin and fry for 30 seconds.

6. Adjust the heat to medium and add 2 tbsps of the tomato purée mixture. Stir and fry until it dries up. Repeat the process until all the tomato purée mixture is used up.

7. Add the warm water and the remaining salt and bring to the boil.

8. Add the koftas, cover the pan and simmer for 10 minutes.

9. Bring the liquid to the boil over a medium heat, stir and cook for 4-5 minutes.

10. Add the peas and the garam masala and continue to cook, uncovered, until the gravy is fairy thick, stirring frequently.

11. Stir in the coriander leaves and remove from the heat.

TIME: Preparation takes 25-30 minutes, cooking takes 50-55 minutes.

SERVING IDEAS: Serve with Pilau Rice or a raita or salad.

MEAT VINDALOO

Vindaloo is made by marinating the meat in vinegar and spices. It is traditionally a hot curry, but the quantity of chillies can be adjusted to suit individual taste.

SERVES 4-6

Grind the following 5 ingredients in a coffee grinder

2 tbsps coriander seeds

1 tbsp cumin seeds

6-8 dried red chillies

1 tbsp mustard seeds

½ tsp fenugreek seeds

3-4 tbsps cider or white wine vinegar

1 tsp ground turmeric

2.5cm/1-inch cube of fresh root ginger, peeled and finely grated

3-4 cloves garlic, crushed

1kg/2¼lbs shoulder of lamb or stewing steak

60ml/4 tbsps cooking oil

1 large onion, finely chopped

1-2 tsps chilli powder

1 tsp paprika

1¼ tsps salt or to taste

430ml/¾ pint warm water

2-3 medium potatoes

1 tbsp chopped coriander leaves, (optional)

1. In a large bowl, make a thick paste out of the ground spices, by adding the vinegar.

2. Add the turmeric, ginger and garlic. Mix thoroughly.

3. Trim off excess fat from the meat and cut into 5cm/1-inch cubes.

4. Add the meat and mix it well so that all the pieces are fully coated with the paste. Cover the bowl with cling film and leave to marinate for 4-6 hours or overnight in the refrigerator.

5. Put the meat in a heavy based pan and place over a medium heat. Allow the meat to heat through, stirring occasionally; this will take about 5 minutes. Cover the pan, and cook the meat in its own juice for 15-20 minutes or until the liquid is reduced to a thick paste. Stir occasionally during this time to ensure that the meat does not stick to the bottom of the pan. Remove from heat and keep aside.

6. Heat the oil over medium heat and fry the onion for about 5 minutes, or until soft.

7. Add the meat and fry for 6-8 minutes stirring frequently.

8. Add the chilli powder, paprika and salt. Stir and fry for a further 2-3 minutes.

9. Add the water, bring to the boil, cover and simmer for 40-45 minutes or until the meat is nearly tender (beef will take longer to cook, check water level and add more water if necessary).

10. Meanwhile, peel and wash the potatoes. Cut them into 4cm/1½-inch cubes. Add this to the meat and bring to the boil again. Cover the pan and simmer for 15-20 minutes, or until the potatoes are cooked.

11. Turn the vindaloo on to a heated serving dish and sprinkle the coriander leaves on top.

TIME: Preparation takes 10-15 minutes plus at least 4 hours for marinating, cooking takes about 1 hour 40 minutes.

ALOO GOSHT

A well-known north-Indian lamb curry with a distinctive flavour imparted by the ghee which is used to brown the potatoes before being added to the curry.

SERVES 4-6

1 × 1kg/2¼lb leg or shoulder of lamb
1¼ tsps salt or to taste
2.5cm/1-inch cube of fresh root ginger, peeled and coarsely chopped
3-4 cloves garlic, coarsely chopped
2 tbsps ghee or unsalted butter
450g/1lb medium potatoes, peeled and cut into 4cm/1½-inch cubes
3 tbsps cooking oil
1 large onion, finely chopped
3-4 dried red chillies
2 cinnamon sticks, broken up

Make a paste of the following 5 spices by adding 3 tbsps water
1 tbsp ground coriander
1 tsp ground allspice
1 tsp paprika
1 tsp ground turmeric
¼-½ tsp chilli powder

1 tbsp tomato purée
2 black cardamoms, split open at the top of each pod
4-6 whole cloves
430ml/¾ pint warm water
1 tbsp lemon juice
2 tbsps chopped coriander leaves

1. Trim off the excess fat from the meat and cut it into 4cm/1½-inch cubes.

2. Add the salt to the ginger and garlic and crush to a pulp.

3. Melt the ghee or butter over a medium heat in a non-stick or cast iron pan and fry the potatoes for about 10 minutes, until they are well-browned on all sides. Remove the potatoes with a slotted spoon and keep aside.

4. Add the oil to any remaining ghee in the pan and when hot, fry the onions, red chillies and cinnamon sticks for about 5 minutes, or until the onions are soft.

5. Add the ginger and garlic pulp, and fry for a further 2-3 minutes stirring frequently.

6. Adjust the heat to low and add the spice paste, stir and fry for 3-4 minutes.

7. Add the meat, stir and fry over a medium high heat for 5-6 minutes until the meat changes colour, then stir in the tomato purée.

8. Now add the cardamoms, cloves and the water. Bring to the boil, cover and simmer for 45-50 minutes.

9. Add the potatoes, bring to the boil again, cover and simmer for 15-20 minutes or until the potatoes are tender.

10. Remove from heat and add the lemon juice and coriander leaves.

TIME: Preparation takes 20-25 minutes, cooking takes 1 hour 30 minutes.

MEAT MADRAS

This hot, but delicious curry is named after Madras, the major city in southern India, perhaps because in the humid south, people eat rather hot food. Strange though it may seem, this is because hot and spicy food makes one perspire, thereby cooling the body.

SERVES 4-6

90ml/6 tbsps oil
2 medium onions, coarsely chopped
2.5cm/1-inch cube of fresh root ginger, peeled and coarsely chopped
3-4 cloves garlic, coarsely chopped
4-6 dried red chillies
2 large cloves garlic, crushed
1-2 fresh green chillies, sliced lengthwise
1 small can of tomatoes
3 tsps ground cumin
1 tsp ground coriander
½-1 tsp chilli powder
1 tsp ground turmeric
1 × 1kg/2¼lb leg or shoulder of lamb, fat removed and cut into 4cm/1½-inch cubes
175ml/6 fl oz warm water
1¼ tsps salt or to taste
1 tsp garam masala

1. Heat 3 tbsps of the oil over a medium heat and fry the onions, coarsely chopped ginger, garlic and red chillies for 8-10 minutes, stirring frequently, until the onions are soft. Remove from the heat and allow to cool.

2. Meanwhile, heat the remaining oil over a medium heat and fry the crushed garlic and green chillies until the garlic is lightly browned.

3. Add half the tomatoes, along with the juice; stir and cook for 1-2 minutes.

4. Add the cumin, coriander, chilli powder and turmeric, over a low heat and cook for 6-8 minutes, stirring frequently.

5. Add the meat, and stir and fry over a medium heat for 5-6 minutes, until meat changes colour.

6. Add the water, bring to the boil, cover and simmer for 30 minutes.

7. Place the fried onion mixture in a blender or food processor and add the remaining tomatoes. Blend until smooth and add this to the meat – bring to the boil, add salt and mix well. Cover the pan and simmer for a further 35-40 minutes or until the meat is tender.

8. Stir in the garam masala and remove from heat.

TIME: Preparation takes 25-30 minutes, cooking takes 1 hour 40 minutes.

SERVING IDEAS: Serve with Plain Boiled Rice or any Indian bread accompanied by a Raita.
Suitable for freezing.

WATCHPOINT: Meat Madras is meant to be hot, but if you like, omit the chilli powder and seed the green chillies.

LAMB CURRY (MILD)

The curry leaves used in this recipe can be found in Oriental stores. Sambal oelek, available in some large supermarkets, is a combination of chillies and salt and is often used in Indonesian cooking.

SERVES 4

1 × 1kg/2¼lb leg of lamb
2 tbsps natural yogurt
1 tbsp sesame oil
2 tsps garam masala
4 cloves garlic, crushed
1 tsp grated ginger
2 tsps curry powder
½ tsp ground black pepper
1 tsp sambal oelek
1 tbsp peanut oil
1 onion, finely sliced
1 tsp dried, crumbled curry leaves
700ml/1¼ pints lamb stock
1 potato, peeled and cut into 1.5cm/½-inch
   dice
3 ripe tomatoes, roughly chopped
2 tbsps desiccated coconut
30g/1oz sultanas
Salt and pepper
1 tbsp desiccated coconut to garnish

1. Cut the lamb into 2.5cm/1-inch cubes.

2. Put the bones in a pan, cover with water, and bring to the boil. Simmer for 10 minutes. Strain and discard the bones.

3. Mix together the yogurt, sesame oil, garam masala, garlic, ginger, curry powder, pepper and sambal oelek. Add the lamb and toss well. Leave to marinate for 30 minutes.

4. Heat a wok, and add the peanut oil. Fry the onion and curry leaves.

5. When softened, increase heat and add the lamb and marinade. Brown the lamb well.

6. Add the lamb stock, potato, tomatoes, desiccated coconut, sultanas, and salt and pepper to taste. Bring to the boil.

7. Reduce the heat, cover and cook gently for 20 minutes. Ensure the potato is covered with liquid (add water if necessary).

8. Remove the lid, and cook for a further 15 minutes. Serve hot, sprinkled with the desiccated coconut.

TIME: Preparation takes 45 minutes including marinating. Cooking takes about 50 minutes.

SERVING IDEAS: Serve with boiled rice and poppadoms.

VARIATION: Use beef or pork instead of lamb in this dish.

PASANDA BADAM CURRY

Pasanda is a classic north Indian dish where the meat is cut into thin slices and cooked in a rich sauce containing saffron, yogurt and cream.

SERVES 4-6

900g/2lbs boned leg of lamb
2.5cm/1-inch cube of fresh root ginger, peeled and coarsely chopped
4-6 cloves garlic, coarsely chopped
2 fresh green chillies, seeded and coarsely chopped
60ml/4 tbsps natural yogurt
60g/2oz ghee or unsalted butter
3 medium onions, finely sliced
½ tsp ground turmeric
1 tsp ground cumin
2 tsps ground coriander
½ tsp ground nutmeg
¼-½ tsp chilli powder
225ml/8 fl oz warm water
1¼ tsps salt or to taste
150ml/5 fl oz single cream
30g/1oz ground almonds
1 tsp garam masala or ground mixed spice
2 tbsps rosewater
½ tsp paprika

1. Beat the meat with a meat mallet to flatten it to 5mm/¼-inch thickness, then cut into thin slices (about 4cm/1½-inch long and 1.25cm/½-inch wide).

2. Put the ginger, garlic, green chillies and yogurt into a liquidiser or food processor and blend until smooth.

3. Melt the ghee or butter over a medium heat and fry the onions for 6-8 minutes or until they are lightly browned.

4. Add the turmeric, cumin, coriander, nutmeg and chilli powder; adjust the heat to low, stir and fry for 2-3 minutes.

5. Add the meat and fry it over high heat for 3-4 minutes or until it changes colour.

6. Add about 2 tbsps of the liquidised ingredients and cook for 1-2 minutes, stirring frequently. Repeat this process until all the yogurt mixture is used up.

7. Now fry the meat over a medium heat for 4-5 minutes stirring frequently. When the fat begins to seep through the thick spice paste and floats on the surface, add the water, bring to the boil, cover the pan and simmer for about 1 hour, or until the meat is tender, stirring occasionally.

8. Add the salt, cream and ground almonds and let it simmer without the lid for 5-6 minutes.

9. Stir in the garam masala and rosewater and remove from heat.

10. Put the pasanda into a heated serving dish and sprinkle the paprika on top.

TIME: Preparation takes 30 minutes, cooking takes 1 hour 15 minutes.

SERVING IDEAS: Serve with Pilau Rice.

VARIATION: Use braising steak.

SHAHI KORMA

The word 'Shahi' means royal, so the title itself is evidence that this particular korma was created in the royal kitchens of the great Maharajas of India. The dish is rich and creamy and is a perfect choice for a special occasion.

SERVES 4-6

1kg/2¼lbs boned leg of lamb, fat trimmed and cut into 4cm/1½-inch cubes

150g/5oz thick set natural yogurt

1.25cm/½-inch cube of root ginger, peeled and grated

3-4 cloves garlic, crushed

60g/2oz ghee or unsalted butter

2 medium onions, finely chopped

Grind the following ingredients in a coffee grinder

2 tbsps coriander seeds

8 whole green cardamoms

10 whole black peppercorns

3-4 dried red chillies

Mix the following 2 spices with the above ground ingredients

1 tsp ground cinnamon

1 tsp ground mace

3-4 tbsps chopped fresh mint or 1½ tsps dried or bottled mint

60g/2oz ground almonds

280ml/½ pint warm water

½ tsp saffron strands, crushed

1½ tsps salt or to taste

60g/2oz split unsalted cashews

150ml/5 fl oz single cream

1 tbsp rosewater

1. Put the meat into a bowl and add the yogurt, ginger and garlic. Mix thoroughly, cover the bowl with cling film and leave to marinate for 2-4 hours or overnight in the refrigerator.

2. Put the marinated meat, along with any remaining marinade, in a heavy-based saucepan over a medium-low heat. Bring to a slow simmer, cover and cook the meat in its own juice for 45-50 minutes, stirring occasionally. Remove the pan from the heat and, using a slotted spoon, transfer the meat to another container and keep hot.

3. Melt the ghee over a medium heat and fry the onions for 8-9 minutes until they are lightly browned.

4. Adjust the heat to low and add the ground ingredients and the mint; stir and fry for 2-3 minutes. Add half of the liquid in which the meat was cooked, stir and cook for 1-2 minutes. Add the ground almonds and mix thoroughly; add the remaining meat stock, stir and cook for a further 1-2 minutes.

5. Adjust heat to medium and add the meat, stir and fry the meat for 5-6 minutes.

6. Add the water, saffron strands, salt and cashews, bring the liquid to a slow boil, cover and simmer for 20 minutes.

7. Add the cream, stir and mix well, and simmer uncovered for 6-8 minutes.

8. Stir in the rosewater and remove from the heat.

GUY'S CURRY (HOT)

This is a hot curry, if you prefer a milder flavour, use a different curry paste.

SERVES 4

60ml/4 tbsps oil
1 onion, finely chopped
3 cloves garlic, chopped
1kg/2lbs steak, skirt or rump, cut into
   1.5cm/½-cubes
2 tbsps sultanas
1 tbsp curry leaves
2 tsps cumin
2 tsps coriander
1 tbsp vindaloo curry paste
1 carrot, grated
1 red pepper, finely chopped
2 apples, finely chopped
2 tomatoes, finely chopped
6 small pieces lemon rind
1 banana, finely sliced
220ml/8 fl oz water
2 tbsps desiccated coconut
2 tsps sugar
340ml/12 fl oz coconut cream

Accompaniments

1 apple, finely chopped
1 banana, sliced
1 red pepper, finely chopped
1 carrot, grated
1 tomato, finely chopped
2 tbsps sultanas
2 tbsps desiccated coconut
Half a cucumber, sliced, in 2 tbsps natural
   yogurt

1. Heat a wok, add the oil and heat until warm.

2. Add the onion and garlic, and fry until golden brown. Remove the garlic, and discard.

3. Add the steak and stir-fry until well browned all over. Add the sultanas and stir in well.

4. Add the curry leaves, stir in, and cook for 5 minutes.

5. Add the cumin and coriander and stir. Cook a further 5 minutes.

6. Add the curry paste and cook for 10 minutes.

7. Add the grated carrot, red pepper, apples, tomatoes, lemon rind and banana and mix in well. Add the water. Cover and cook for 30 minutes.

8. Stir in the desiccated coconut and cook for a further 30 minutes.

9. Add the sugar and cook for another 20 minutes. Add more water as necessary.

10. Add the coconut cream and cook a further 20 minutes. Serve hot with the prepared accompaniments.

Meat Durbari

The word 'Durbar' means forum or formal gathering. This wonderful lamb dish originated in the royal kitchens and was served at special gatherings held by the great Mughal Emperors.

SERVES 4

1 × 1kg/2¼lb leg of lamb

Grind the following 9 ingredients in a coffee grinder and make a paste by adding the vinegar

1 tbsp mustard seeds

1 tbsp sesame seeds

2 tbsps white poppy seeds

10 black peppercorns

2-4 dried red chillies

1 bay leaf

5cm/2-inch piece of cinnamon stick, broken

4 whole cloves

Seeds of 2 black cardamoms

3 tbsps white wine vinegar

1¼ tsp salt

3-4 cloves garlic, coarsely chopped

3 tbsps ghee or unsalted butter

1 large onion, finely chopped

2.5cm/1-inch cube of fresh root ginger, peeled and finely grated

175ml/6 fl oz warm water

1 tbsp tomato purée

2 fresh green chillies, slit lengthwise into halves, seeded for a milder flavour

2 tbsps chopped coriander leaves

1. Trim off excess fat from the meat and cut into 5cm/2-inch cubes.

2. Rub the spice paste well into the meat and leave to marinate for 4-6 hours, or overnight in the refrigerator.

3. Add the salt to the garlic and crush to a smooth pulp.

4. Melt the ghee or butter gently over a low heat, add the onion and ginger, and sauté over a medium heat for 3-4 minutes, or until the onions are soft.

5. Add the garlic paste and fry for a further 2-3 minutes stirring frequently.

6. Add the meat and cook, in the onion mixture, until all sides of meat are sealed and brown.

7. Add the water, bring to the boil, cover and simmer for 50-60 minutes or until the meat is tender.

8. Add the tomato purée, green chillies and coriander leaves and cook over a medium heat for 3-4 minutes, stirring continuously. Remove the pan from the heat.

TIME: Preparation takes 20-25 minutes plus at least 4 hours marinating, cooking takes 1 hour 10 minutes.

KOFTA CURRY

Use either lamb or beef mince to make the meat balls or koftas in this recipe.

SERVES 4

450g/1lb lean mince
½ tsp ginger paste
1 tsp garlic paste
1 egg
1 tsp ground garam masala
½ tsp chilli powder

For sauce

1 onion, finely chopped
30-45g/1-1½oz ghee or 2-3 tbsps oil
6 small cardamoms
2.5cm/1-inch stick cinnamon
6 cloves
1 bayleaf
1 tsp garlic paste
1 tsp ginger paste
1 tsp ground cumin
½ tsp chilli powder
¼ tsp turmeric powder
2 tsp ground coriander
140ml/¼ pint natural yogurt or 2 tbsps
    tomato purée
570ml/1 pint water
Salt to taste

Garnish

2 green chillies, chopped
2 sprigs fresh coriander, finely chopped

1. Mix the mince with the ginger, garlic paste and egg. Add the garam masala and chilli powder.

2. Mix well and make 16-20 even-sized balls. Keep refrigerated.

3. Fry the onion in ghee for 4 minutes until light golden brown. Add the cardamom, cinnamon, cloves and bayleaf. Stir and fry for 1 minute.

4. Add the garlic and ginger pastes and fry for another minute. Sprinkle with the cumin, chilli, turmeric and coriander.

5. Stir well and add the yogurt or tomato purée. If yogurt is used, fry the spices for 5-7 minutes, until yogurt is dry and the oil separates.

6. Add the water, cover and bring to boil. Add salt. Slide the koftas one at a time, into the saucepan.

7. Shake the saucepan to settle the koftas; do not stir else they will break up. Cover and gently simmer for 20 minutes.

8. Garnish with chopped chillies and coriander leaves.

TIME: Preparation takes 15 minutes, cooking takes about 30 minutes.

KORMA

Korma is a classic north Indian dish and there are many variations, some of which are quite elaborate. The recipe below however, is simple and easily prepared.

SERVES 4

1 medium onion, thinly sliced
45g/1½oz ghee or 3 tbsps oil
2.5cm/1-inch cinnamon stick
6 cloves
6 small cardamoms
1 bayleaf
1 tsp nigella or black cumin seeds
2 tsp ginger paste
1 tsp garlic paste
450g/1lb shoulder of lamb, cubed
1 tsp chilli powder
1 tsp ground coriander
2 tsp ground cumin
¼ tsp turmeric powder
140ml/¼ pint natural yogurt
175ml/6 fl oz water
Salt to taste
1 tbsp ground almonds
2 green chillies, halved
2 sprigs fresh coriander, chopped

1. Fry the onion in the ghee or oil until golden brown. Add the cinnamon, cloves, cardamoms, bayleaf and black cumin. Fry for 1 minute, add the ginger and garlic paste. Stir for half a minute.

2. Add the meat and sprinkle with the chilli, coriander, cumin and turmeric powders.

3. Mix well and add the yogurt. Cover and cook for 10-15 minutes, occasionally stirring the mixture.

4. Add the water, salt to taste and cover. Cook on a low heat for 30-40 minutes or until meat is tender.

5. Add the ground almonds, green chillies and coriander leaves. Add extra water if needed.

TIME: Preparation takes about 15 minutes and cooking takes about 45-55 minutes.

COOK'S TIP: A korma should have a medium-thick gravy.

BUYING GUIDE: Nigella or kalonji, to give it its Indian name is available from Oriental stores.

PLAIN BOILED RICE

Rice cookery needs no special technique, but a few simple rules will produce perfect results every time. Do not lift the lid while the rice is cooking. Do not stir the rice at any stage during cooking or immediately after it has been removed from the heat. This will ensure dry and separate grains every time.

SERVES 4-6

280g/10oz basmati or other long grain rice, washed and soaked in cold water for 30 minutes
510ml/18 fl oz water
½ tsp salt
1 tsp ghee or butter

1. Drain the rice thoroughly and put into a saucepan with the water.

2. Bring to the boil, stir in the salt and the ghee.

3. Place the lid on the saucepan and simmer: 12 minutes for basmati rice, 15 minutes for other long grain rice.

4. Remove from the heat and keep the pot covered for a further 10-12 minutes.

5. Fork through the rice gently before serving. Use a metal serving spoon as wooden ones tend to squash the grains.

TIME: Preparation takes 30 minutes, cooking takes 12-15 minutes. Stand for 10-12 minutes before serving.

SERVING IDEAS: Plain Boiled Rice can be served with any curry. Suitable for freezing.

VARIATION: Garnish with fried onion rings or fresh coriander leaves.

PILAU RICE

Pilau is usually a beautifully fragrant rice or a combination of rice and meat, poultry, fish or vegetables. It is always cooked in pure butterfat ghee, but unsalted butter is a good substitute.

SERVES 4-6

280g/10oz basmati rice
60g/2oz ghee or unsalted butter
1 large onion, finely sliced
2-4 cloves garlic, finely chopped
8 whole cloves
8 green cardamoms, split open at the top of each pod
2 cinnamon sticks, 5cm/2-inches long each, broken up
8 whole peppercorns
1 tsp ground turmeric
570ml/1 pint water
1¼ tsps salt or to taste
Nut of butter
30g/1oz seedless sultanas
30g/1oz flaked almonds

1. Wash the rice and soak in cold water for 30 minutes. Drain well.

2. In a heavy-based pan melt the ghee or butter over a medium heat and fry the onion for about 5 minutes, until soft but not brown.

3. Add the garlic, cloves, cardamoms, cinnamon sticks and peppercorns. Stir and fry for 3-4 minutes, or until the onions are golden brown.

4. Add the rice and turmeric, stir and fry for 1-2 minutes. Adjust the heat to low, stir and fry the rice for a further 2-3 minutes.

5. Add the water and the salt, bring to the boil, cover and simmer for 15 minutes without lifting the lid.

6. Remove the pan from heat and keep it undisturbed for a further 10-12 minutes.

7. Melt the butter over a gentle heat and cook the sultanas for 1 minute or until they change colour and swell up. Transfer the sultanas onto a plate and then brown the almonds. Remove to a separate plate.

8. Put the pilau rice into a serving dish and, using a fork, gently mix in the fried sultanas and almonds.

TIME: Preparation takes 10 minutes plus 30 minutes needed to soak the rice. Cooking takes 25-30 minutes plus 10-12 minutes standing time.

SERVING IDEAS: Serve with Chicken Korma or a Chicken Tikka Masala. Suitable for freezing.

VARIATION: Omit the almonds and use a hard-boiled sliced egg to garnish.

CURRIED RICE SALAD

Curry powder and a tangy mayonnaise dressing makes this rice salad a bit different.

SERVES 6

175g/6oz long grain rice
1 tbsp curry powder, hot or mild
4 spring onions, sliced
2 sticks celery, sliced
1 small green pepper, diced
10 black olives, halved and pitted
60g/2oz sultanas
60g/2oz toasted flaked almonds
22g/4 tbsps flaked coconut
2 hard-boiled eggs, chopped

Dressing
140ml/¼ pint mayonnaise
1 tbsp mango chutney
Juice and grated rind of ½ lime
60ml/4 tbsps natural yogurt
Salt

Garnish
2 avocados, peeled and cut in cubes
Juice of ½ lemon or lime

1. Cook the rice in boiling salted water for about 12 minutes or until just tender. During the last 3 minutes of cooking stir in the curry powder.

2. Leave to continue cooking over a gentle heat until the rice is just cooked and the water is evaporated.

3. Turn the rice out onto a large platter. Toss the rice with a fork to spread out and leave to cool.

4. Combine with the remaining salad ingredients, stirring carefully so that the hard-boiled eggs do not break up.

5. Mix the dressing ingredients together thoroughly, finely chopping any large pieces of mango in the chutney.

6. Stir the dressing into the salad and using two forks, gently toss to coat. Arrange the rice salad in a mound on a serving dish.

7. Sprinkle the cubed avocado with the lemon juice to keep it green and place around the rice salad before serving.

TIME: Preparation takes about 20 minutes and cooking takes about 12 minutes.

KASHMIRI DUM ALOO

*This is a lovely way to serve new potatoes. The potatoes are boiled,
then fried until they are golden brown, and finally simmered gently
in natural yogurt and spices.*

SERVES 4

560g/1¼lbs small new potatoes
2 tbsps ghee or unsalted butter
1 tsp fennel seeds

Mix the following 5 ingredients in a small bowl
½ tsp ground cumin
1 tsp ground coriander
¼ tsp freshly ground black pepper
½ tsp ground turmeric
½ tsp ground ginger

150g/5oz thick set natural yogurt
1 tsp salt or to taste
¼ tsp garam masala
1 tbsp chopped coriander leaves
1 fresh green chilli, seeded and finely
    chopped

---

1. Boil the potatoes in their jackets, cool and peel them. Prick the potatoes all over to enable the spices to penetrate deep inside.

2. Melt the ghee over a medium heat in a non-stick or cast iron pan.

3. When the ghee is hot, fry the potatoes in a single layer for about 8-10 minutes, or until they are well browned, turning them over frequently. Remove them with a slotted spoon and set aside.

4. Remove the pan from the heat and stir in the fennel seeds followed by the spice mixture. Adjust the heat to low and place the pan back on the heat, stir the spices and fry for 1 minute.

5. Add the yogurt and salt, and mix well. Add the potatoes, cover the pan and simmer for 10-12 minutes. Add the garam masala and remove the pan from the heat.

6. Stir in the coriander leaves and the green chilli.

TIME: Preparation takes 30-35 minutes including boiling the potatoes,
cooking takes 20-25 minutes.

SERVING IDEAS: Serve as a side dish with Chicken Korma, or Murghi
Badami.

WATCHPOINT: Do not use a steel or enamel pan for browning the
potatoes or they will stick to the pan and break up.

Toorai Tarkari (Courgette Curry)

This courgette dish makes a good accompaniment to a main course curry.

SERVES 3-4

1½ tbsps oil

1 tsp cumin seeds

225g/8oz courgettes, sliced into 5mm/
    ¼-inch thick rounds

½ tsp chilli powder

1 tsp ground coriander

¼ tsp turmeric powder

3-4 fresh or canned tomatoes, chopped

Salt to taste

1 green chilli, halved

1 sprig fresh coriander leaves, chopped

1. Heat the oil and add the cumin seeds. When they crackle, add the courgette slices.

2. Stir and sprinkle with the chilli, coriander and turmeric powder.

3. Mix well and add the chopped tomatoes. Sprinkle with salt, the green chilli and fresh coriander.

4. Cover and cook for 10-12 minutes.

TIME: Preparation takes 10 minutes and cooking takes about 15 minutes.

COOK'S TIP: If using fresh tomatoes, remove the skins first.

ALOO CHOLE

Chick peas are delicious cooked with spices and diced potatoes. They do need prolonged cooking before they are tender. It is worth cooking them in the pressure cooker, if you have one, as it will only take 20 minutes with 15lbs pressure.

SERVES 4-6

225g/8oz chick peas, picked over and washed

850ml/1½ pints water

1.25cm/½-inch cube of fresh root ginger, peeled and grated

1 large waxy potato, peeled and cut into 4cm/1½-inch cubes

1 tsp ground cumin

½ tsp ground turmeric

¼-½ tsp chilli powder, optional

1-2 fresh green chillies, slit lengthwise into halves; seeded for a milder flavour

30g/1oz ghee or unsalted butter

1 large onion, finely chopped

1¼ tsp salt or to taste

½ tsp garam masala

1 tbsp lemon juice

1 tbsp chopped fresh mint or 1 tsp dried mint

1. Soak the chick peas overnight in plenty of cold water. Rinse several times and drain well.

2. Put the chick peas, water and ginger into a saucepan and place over a high heat, bring to the boil, cover the pan and simmer for 1¼-1½ hours or until the peas are tender. Alternatively, put the peas and the ginger in a pressure cooker and add 430ml/¾ pint water. Bring to the boil, then following the usual method for pressure cooking, cook under pressure for 20 minutes. Stand the pressure cooker aside until pressure is reduced.

3. Add the potatoes, cumin, turmeric, chilli powder and the green chillies, and the mint, if you are using it dried. Bring to the boil again, cover the pan and simmer for a further 15-20 minutes or until the potatoes are tender.

4. Melt the ghee over medium heat and fry the onion until they are lightly browned (6-8 minutes). Stir this into the chick peas along with the salt and garam masala.

5. Remove the pan from heat and stir in the lemon juice and fresh mint.

TIME: Preparation takes 10-15 minutes plus overnight soaking for the peas, cooking takes 1½-1¾ hours.

SERVING IDEAS: Serve with puris or as a side dish with meat/fish/chicken curry. Avoid serving with rich and creamy curries.

TO FREEZE: Suitable for freezing, but freeze before adding the potatoes.

NEW POTATO FRY

This Oriental dish is very versatile; it can be served as a side dish, as a snack, or, as a main curry.

SERVES 3-4

3 tbsps oil
1 tsp mustard seed
450g/1lb small, even sized new potatoes, boiled in their skins and peeled
1 tsp red chilli powder
1½ tsps ground coriander
¼ tsp ground turmeric
½ tsp salt
3 sprigs fresh coriander leaves chopped (optional)
Lemon juice to taste

1. Heat the oil in a wok or heavy based frying pan and add the mustard seed and the whole, peeled potatoes.

2. Stir fry over a low heat until they are lightly browned.

3. Sprinkle with the spices, salt and chopped coriander leaves.

4. Stir over a low heat for 5-6 minutes until golden brown. Remove from the heat.

5. Put into a dish and sprinkle with the lemon juice. Serve hot or cold.

TIME: Preparation takes about 20 minutes, and cooking takes about 15-20 minutes.

COOK'S TIP: Try substituting large cooked potatoes and cutting them into large dice. Use a waxy variety for best results.

CAULIFLOWER MASALA

This dish, with potatoes and peas, is flavoured with a few basic ingredients and the finished dish is semi-dry, making it an ideal accompaniment to rice and curry or Indian bread.

SERVES 4-6

1 medium cauliflower
2 medium potatoes
60ml/4 tbsps cooking oil
1 tsp cumin seeds
1 large onion
½ tsp ground turmeric
1 tsp ground coriander
1 tsp ground cumin
¼-½ tsp chilli powder
2 ripe tomatoes, skinned and chopped
175ml/6 fl oz warm water
120g/4oz shelled peas, fresh or frozen
   (cook fresh peas until they are tender
   before using)
1-2 fresh green chillies, seeded and slit
   lengthwise into halves
1 tsp salt
½ tsp garam masala
1 tbsp chopped coriander leaves

1. Cut the cauliflower into 1.25cm/½-inch diameter florets – wash and drain.

2. Peel and cut the potatoes lengthwise into 1.25cm/½-inch thick strips.

3. Heat the oil over a medium heat and add the cumin seeds. As soon as they start popping, add the onion and fry for about 5 minutes, or until soft.

4. Turn the heat down to low and add the turmeric, coriander, cumin and chilli powder. Stir and fry for 2-3 minutes and add the chopped tomatoes. Fry for a further 2-3 minutes stirring continuously.

5. Add the potatoes and the water. Bring to the boil, cover the pan and simmer until the potatoes are half-cooked.

6. Add the cauliflower, cover the pan again and simmer for about 10 minutes, until the potatoes are tender.

7. Stir in the peas, green chillies, salt and garam masala. Cover and cook for 5 minutes.

8. Remove from heat and stir in the coriander leaves.

TIME: Preparation takes about 25 minutes, cooking takes 30-35 minutes.

VARIATION: Cook in 45g/1½oz ghee instead of oil for a richer flavour.

Index